JESUS' STORIES

A Family Parable Devotional

Carine
Mackenzie

Illustrated by
Nicoletta Ranieri

CF4·K

10 9 8 7 6 5 4 3 2 1

Copyright © 2024 Carine MacKenzie

ISBN: 978-1-5271-1102-8

Published by Christian Focus Publications,

Geanies House, Fearn, Tain, Ross-shire, IV20 1TW, U.K.

Illustrations by Nicoletta Ranieri
Design by Pete Barnsley (CreativeHoot.com)

Printed and bound in Malaysia

This book
belongs to:

....

Contents

Why did Jesus Tell Parables?

We all love to listen to stories. Perhaps you like to tell stories to your friends and family.

Jesus used powerful stories, called parables, to help his followers understand more about the truths of God.

In the parables he talked about everyday sights and activities to illustrate his teachings.

This method made his teaching easy to remember for those who were interested. Some unbelievers who were not interested, could not grasp the spiritual meaning of Jesus' parables.

Jesus' stories are for us today too. What kind of listener are you?

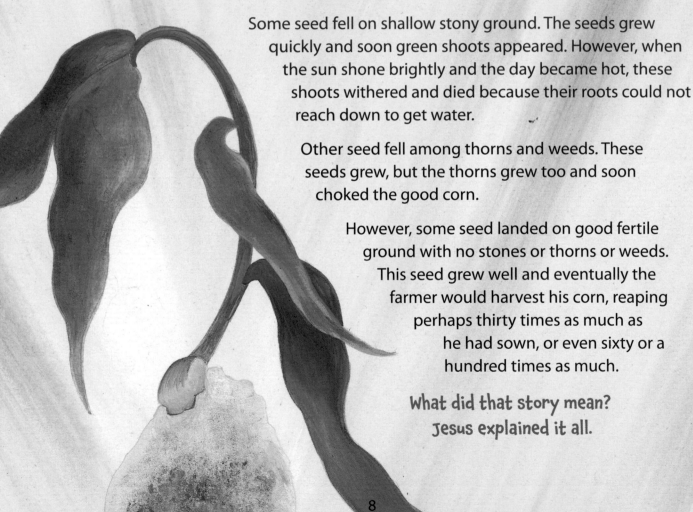

The Sower

Matthew 13:1-23

Jesus told a story to show how people listen differently to God's Word.

A farmer went out to sow seed in his field, throwing handfuls of seed to the right and to the left. Some seed fell on the pathway. Soon the birds came and ate it all up.

Some seed fell on shallow stony ground. The seeds grew quickly and soon green shoots appeared. However, when the sun shone brightly and the day became hot, these shoots withered and died because their roots could not reach down to get water.

Other seed fell among thorns and weeds. These seeds grew, but the thorns grew too and soon choked the good corn.

However, some seed landed on good fertile ground with no stones or thorns or weeds. This seed grew well and eventually the farmer would harvest his corn, reaping perhaps thirty times as much as he had sown, or even sixty or a hundred times as much.

What did that story mean? Jesus explained it all.

8

The seed is like the Word of God. This seed is sown when we hear God's Word read or preached or when we read it for ourselves.

9

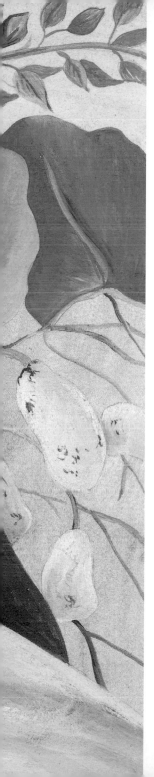

Some people hear God's Word, but soon the devil comes and takes the Word away from their minds. They forget God's Word and do not believe the gospel. That is like the seed pecked away by the birds.

Other people hear God's Word gladly. They believe for a while, but when trouble comes or if someone mocks them for being interested in God and his Word, then their interest withers away. It is not deeply rooted in God. This situation is like the seed sown on stony ground.

There are other people who hear the Word of God and seem to be making good progress. However, soon the cares about money and pleasure take over their thoughts and their interest in the Bible is choked out. These cares and pleasures are like weeds and thorns. They choke the good Word which then does not produce a good result.

The seed on the good ground is like the person who hears the Word of God and loves it and obeys it. The Word brings fruit in their lives – fruit like love, joy, peace, patience. This fruit is only produced by the power of the Holy Spirit. Their lives are made new.

In each situation the seed is the same. The Word of God never changes. It is always true and without error. People hear the Word differently, just as their souls are different. Those who preach God's Word do not know how the Word will be received.

Their duty is to preach the truth to everyone.
Only God can make the word grow in your heart.

The House Builders

Matthew 7:24-27

We all need houses to live in. Two men each had to build a house for himself and his family. Both wanted them to be safe and strong.

One wise man built his house on a rock which was a good firm foundation. When the storm and rain came, the house was warm and safe.

Jesus said that if we hear what God tells us in the Bible, and put it into practice in our lives, we are like the wise man in the parable. Our lives will be secure on a solid foundation and will stand up to the storms and difficulties of life.

However, if we hear God's Word and do not do what he tells us, then we are like a foolish man. He built his house on a foundation of sand. When the storms came, the foundation slipped, the bricks moved out of place and soon the house was in ruins.

If we do not obey God's Word, our lives will be in ruins too.

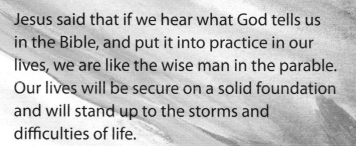

13

The Rich Fool

(Luke 12:16–21)

Jesus told a story to show
that we do not have
to be rich to belong
to his kingdom.

A rich man owned a lot of good farmland. His farm was prosperous and produced a large amount of grain.

He thought, 'My barns are not big enough to store all this grain. What will I do with it? I do not want to give it away. I want to keep it all for myself.' How selfish he was.

So he pulled down his barns and built bigger ones. He felt pleased with himself. 'I am well off. I can take things easy and do just as I please,' he said to himself.

However, that night he died and lost all his possessions. He actually had nothing. Was he really a happy man? No. Jesus calls him a fool.

If we are greedy and store up things for ourselves, we are fools too. We have to leave this world one day and meet with God, our Judge. The important things in life are not the things we own.

The most important thing is that we have love in our heart to the Lord Jesus and that we love other people.

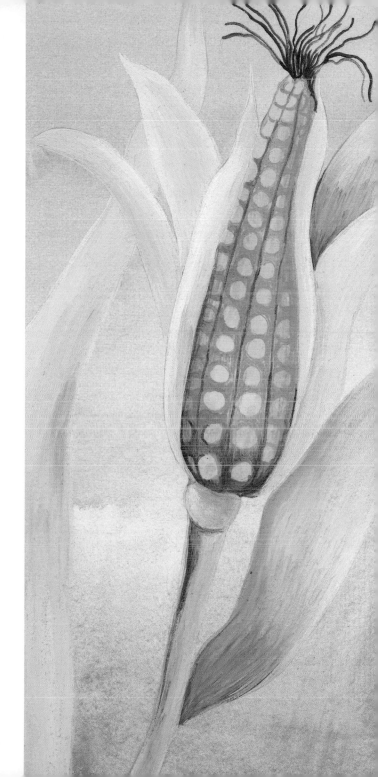

Let's Pray!

Ask God to help you learn from
the Bible and believe the
words written there.

Ask him to help you listen to
his Word and obey it.

Thank God for his love for you and
ask him to help you love others.

Ten Girls at a Wedding

Matthew 25:1-13

Jesus wants us to know that those who belong to his kingdom need the help of the Holy Spirit.

He told a story about a wedding. The custom then was for the bridegroom to arrive late at the bride's house. Her friends, or bridesmaids, would go out to meet him and escort him with lamps into the bride's house.

One girl had ten bridesmaids. Five of these girls were wise; they had brought plenty of oil for their lamps. Five of them were foolish. They did not take any extra oil with them.

The bridegroom was a long time in coming, so they all dropped off to sleep. At midnight, someone shouted, 'The bridegroom is on his way. Get ready to meet him.'

All the girls woke up and got their lamps ready.

'Our lamps are beginning to go out,' wailed the five foolish girls. 'We have not got enough oil. Give us some of yours.'

'Not at all,' the wise ones replied. 'We might not have enough for both us and you. Go to the merchant and buy for yourselves.'

So off they went to buy more oil. While they were away, the bridegroom arrived. The five wise girls greeted him and went into the bride's house. The door was then shut.

Later the other girls arrived.

'Sir, sir, let us in!' they shouted.

'Certainly not,' replied the bridegroom. 'You are too late.'

The oil is like the Holy Spirit who lives inside the followers of Jesus. He helps them to shine brightly for Jesus.

Wheat and Weeds

Matthew 13:24-30; 36-43

Jesus knew that his enemy, the devil, would try to destroy his kingdom. He told a story to make this clear.

A farmer sowed good seed in his field.

One night, while everyone was asleep, an enemy came and sowed weeds among his good wheat seeds. He hurried off before anyone saw him. The farmer did not suspect anything until the plants began to grow. Only then did the weeds show up. The farm workers were concerned about the weeds.

'Where have they come from?' they asked.

'One of my enemies must have done this,' the farmer replied.

'Will we go and pull out the weeds?' the farm hands asked.

'No,' replied the farmer. 'You might pull up some wheat as well. Let both wheat and weeds grow together until harvest time. I will tell the workers to harvest the weeds first, tie them in bundles and burn them. Then the wheat will be safely gathered into the barn.'

Jesus explained to his disciples exactly what he meant by this story.

The Lord Jesus himself is represented by the farmer who sowed the seed. The field is the world. The good seeds are the people who belong to the kingdom of Jesus. The enemy is the devil and the wicked people who belong to him.

The harvest happens at the Day of Judgement. The angels are the reapers. Those who belong to the devil will then be destroyed forever.

Those who love the Lord will be gathered by him to be in heaven where they will be perfectly blessed and happy.

A Mustard Seed

Matthew 13:31-32

Jesus used little things to show what his kingdom is.

He used the mustard seed to show that his kingdom is growing.

The mustard seed is exceptionally tiny, but when it is sown in the ground, it grows into a big tree – so big that birds can even build nests in it.

Jesus' kingdom had a small beginning, but has grown and will continue to grow.

Jesus used yeast as the object of a story to show that Jesus' kingdom has an effect.

When a woman is making bread, she uses a tiny amount of yeast in the flour. This makes a huge batch of dough rise.

Without the yeast the bread would be flat and hard. The yeast is not seen, but its effect is certainly noticed.

Yeast

Matthew 13:33

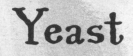

When someone belongs to the kingdom of Jesus, the change in their life will certainly be noticeable.

Let's Pray!

Ask God the Holy Spirit to help you give glory to God, that your life will show others what God is like.

Thank God for his Son Jesus Christ. Ask him to help you trust in him.

Thank God that his Kingdom is growing. Ask him to help you tell others about him.

Say sorry to God for the wrong you have done and ask him to forgive and change you.

A Hidden Treasure

Matthew 13:44

What does the story of the hidden treasure teach us? It teaches us that Jesus' kingdom is worth everything.

A man discovered that treasure was hidden in a field. He rushed off to buy that field for himself. He had to sell everything else that he owned in order to afford to buy the field. He was so happy when the field and the treasure belonged to him.

Belonging to the kingdom is most precious and worth giving up everything else.

A Costly Pearl

Matthew 13:45–46

Jesus' kingdom of
Heaven is precious.

There was a man who saw an
extremely beautiful pearl for
sale. He wanted it so much that
he thought it was worth selling
everything else he had in order to be
able to buy the pearl!

Belonging to the kingdom of
Jesus is more important
than anything else.

Fishing Net

Matthew 13:47-50

With this story Jesus is teaching us that he knows who belongs to his kingdom.

When the fisherman pulls in the fishing net he catches all sorts of fish. At the shore he divides the catch into good fish, which go into a bucket to be used, and bad fish which are thrown away as useless.

Jesus told this story to remind us that at the end of time he will separate those who are in his kingdom from those who are not.

Jesus tells that the most important thing to do is to enter his kingdom. He says that if we ask God for mercy he will forgive us our sin. Our greatest sin is to reject Jesus' salvation which is offered to us.

The religious leaders, the Pharisees, complained when Jesus made friends with tax collectors and sinners. But these people were important to Jesus. He explained this to the Pharisees with interesting stories.

The Lost Sheep

Luke 15:1-7

A man has one hundred sheep. If one gets lost, what will he do? Will he not leave the other ninety-nine sheep safely grazing and go searching for the lost sheep? He will not give up until he finds it.

How happy he will be, carrying home his stray sheep on his shoulders. This newly found sheep will be a cause for celebration. Friends and neighbours will join in.

In the same way there is joy in heaven each time Jesus finds a lost sinner. Jesus does not want anyone to be lost. He longs for us to be in his kingdom.

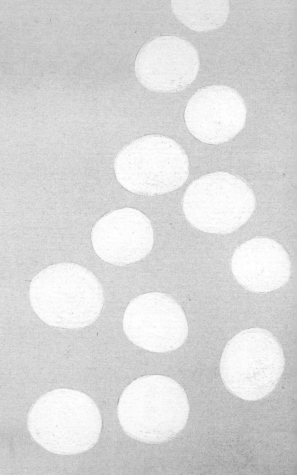

Let's Pray!

Thank God for the Bible. Ask him to help you realise how precious it is.

Ask God to save you from your sins. Repent of the wrong things you have done, said and thought.

Thank God that he is willing to rescue you from sin. Ask him to bring you into his family.

The Lost Coin

Luke 15:8-10

Jesus then told a story of a woman who had ten precious silver coins.

One day something was wrong. One of the coins was missing. What would she do? Just forget about it? Certainly not.

She lit the lamp to brighten up the room, fetched her brush and began to sweep every corner of the house. She swept and swept until at last she caught sight of the missing coin in a corner.

How pleased she was. She shouted to her friends and neighbours, 'I have found my lost coin! Isn't it great?' Her friends were so happy for her.

Jesus wants us to know that the angels in heaven are happy when one lost sinner is found by him. Jesus has taken every care to make sure that we would be safe with him in his kingdom.

The Lost Sons

Luke 15:11-32

A father had two sons. The older boy worked on his father's farm. The younger one wanted to leave home and go far away to enjoy himself. One day he said to his father, 'Half of your money will be mine one day. Can I have it now?'

A few days later the young man left home with his father's money. He travelled a long way from home. He had plenty of money to spend on food and drink and parties. He had plenty of friends to help him spend the money, but when the money was used up these friends disappeared. The young man was left alone.

Famine came to the land. Instead of enjoying plenty of food and fun with his companions, the young man had nothing and was hungry – no food – no friends – no family.

'I'll need to find a job,' he thought. A pig farmer hired him to look after his pigs – a common and dirty job. He was so hungry he felt like eating the husks of corn that the pigs were eating. He was miserable. At last he came to his senses. 'Here I am starving,' he thought, 'while even the servants in my father's house have plenty to eat. I will go back to my father. I will admit that I have sinned against him and against God. I will ask to be one of his servants, for I am not worthy to be his son.'

So he set off for home. Would his father turn him away?

While he was still a good distance from the house, he noticed a figure running down the road to greet him. It was his father! He must have been looking out for him, hoping he would return. 'Oh, Father,' the boy said. 'I have sinned against heaven and against you, and am not worthy to be your son.' The young man expressed his repentance and sorrow for his sin and his father listened.

When we express repentance and sorrow for our sin from our heart, then God listens and welcomes us to himself. Repentance is a gift from the Lord God through Jesus Christ. Only through his death on the cross can we receive forgiveness of sins.

The father not only listened to his son, but forgave him freely. He called to one of his servants, 'Bring out the best robe. Put a ring on his hand and shoes on his feet. Prepare a special meal with a fatted calf. Let's celebrate. It was as if my son was dead, but now he is alive. He was lost, but is now found.' So, a big party began.

The older son had been working hard in the field all day. When he came near the house, he heard the sound of music and dancing.

'What's all the noise about?' he shouted to a servant.

'It's good news,' the servant replied. 'Your brother has come home. Your father has ordered a celebration.'

The older brother was so angry, he would not go into the house. The father came out to reason with him.

'You have never made a party for me and my friends and I have worked for you for years. But as soon as this waster comes home you make a special celebration for him,' he complained.

What a disappointment for the father. This son showed no love. Even although he had not left home as his brother did, he was working just out of duty and not with love.

'All that I have is yours. It is right to rejoice that your brother has returned,' reasoned the father.

This parable of Jesus points us to our loving Father God.

Some of us can rebel and go far from the ways of God. Others can outwardly belong to the church, but serve God grudgingly.

Both types of people need to repent. God the Father has such love for the world that he sent his Son to live and die for us.

The Wedding Feast

Matthew 22:1-14

Jesus tells us that we only enter his kingdom one way.

A king prepared a wonderful wedding feast for his son. Lovely food was made. The invitations were sent out. But the guests refused to come.

'I am too busy; I must attend to my farm. Please excuse me,' said one.

'I cannot come; I must try out my new oxen,' said another. 'Do accept my apologies.'

Some others were not so polite. They grabbed the servants who had brought the invitation and beat them up and murdered them.

How ungrateful and wicked.

The king was angry, so he sent his soldiers to deal out justice to these evil murderers.

The wedding feast was ready and waiting.

'The people I invited do not deserve to come. We will find other guests to celebrate my son's marriage,' he said.

'Go out into the streets,' ordered the king, 'and invite any poor person you find. They are welcome to the feast.'

The servants went out and gathered everyone they could find – good or bad, poor, crippled, or blind. Eventually the feast had plenty of guests.

This story is a picture of God the Father asking sinners to believe in his Son, Jesus, and share the blessings he provides. Sadly, most who are asked, refuse. They all have excuses. Yet some do believe. Jesus turns nobody away.

In Bible times the host always provided a special wedding garment for each guest. As the king was walking round his guests, he spotted one man without the special wedding garment. 'How did you get in here without the wedding garment?' he asked.

The man could not utter a word. He had thought his own clothes were good enough. He was immediately thrown out of the feast into the darkness.

Jesus' salvation is like the wedding garment. Jesus has provided us with suitable covering for all our sins. This is his own righteousness which he gives to all who trust in him.

When we trust in Jesus, we have entered the kingdom of God.

The Pharisee and the Tax Collector

Luke 18:9-14

Two men went up to the temple to pray.

One man was a Pharisee – he was most particular about keeping the law in every detail. The other man was a tax collector. The people did not like tax collectors. Many of them were dishonest and collected too much money.

The Pharisee was proud of himself and thought he was so good. When he prayed, he told God how good he was. 'Thank you, God, that I am not greedy or dishonest or immoral like other people. I am not like that tax collector over there. I fast twice a week. I give one tenth of all my income to you.' He was smug and pleased with himself.

The tax collector was quite different. He knew he was a sinner and that God was holy. He stood with his head bowed and said humbly, 'God have mercy on me, a sinner.'

This was a real prayer from his heart. Jesus tells us that the tax collector was forgiven by God, but the Pharisee was not.

It is not how good we think we are that matters. We must see that we are sinners and ask God to show mercy to us. When we do this, we enter his kingdom.

Let's Pray!

Thank God for his love and care for you. Thank him for wanting you to be safe with him in his Kingdom.

Repent of your sins. Thank God for his love and mercy.

Ask God to show you where you are sinning. Ask God to show you how wonderful he is.

The Three Servants

Matthew 25:14-30

Once we have trusted in Jesus and are part of his kingdom we are asked to live every day for him. We can serve him in many different ways. In his parables, Jesus showed how we can do this.

A wealthy man had to go on a long journey. He called his servants and entrusted them with some of his property.

To one he gave five talents of money, to another, two and to a third, one. A talent was worth a lot of money. He wanted them to use the money wisely for him.

While the master was away the first servant used the money, traded and made good profits, so when the master returned, he told him, 'I have increased your talents to ten talents now.'

'Well done!' said the master. 'You have been good and faithful in this small matter. I will reward you and put you in charge of much more.'

The second servant had also used his talents wisely. He doubled the master's money and was rewarded for his faithfulness.

However, the third servant was not sensible. He simply dug a hole in the ground and buried the money. When the master came back, he said, 'Here is your money back. I was afraid that I would lose it and I knew that would make you angry.'

44

'You lazy servant!' shouted the master. 'Could you not at least have put the money in the bank and then it would have earned interest. You are not capable of looking after anything. Your talent will be given to the first servant who has proved that he is faithful.'

We do not have money called talents, but we do have other kinds of talents which God expects us to use for him.

We should use what Jesus has given us for his service. Even the smallest thing that we do should be done for him.

Two Sons in the Vineyard

Matthew 21:28-32

Jesus told a story about a man who had two sons.

One day the father said to the older boy,
'I need your help, son. Go and work in the
vineyard for me.'

'No, I don't want to,' he answered. However, later he was
sorry for what he had said and went to work in the vineyard.

The father also went to the younger son and asked him to go and work
in the vineyard.

'Yes sir, of course,' he replied right away, sounding so willing to
help, but he did not even turn up at the vineyard.

Which boy did what his father wanted? The older one. He did
wrong at first, but then he repented.

Jesus is teaching us that our actions are more
important than all the fine words that we say.
Those who obey the Lord Jesus show that
they are in his kingdom.

Workers in the Vineyard

Matthew 20:1-16

Jesus told another story to show what his kingdom is like.

A landowner went out early one morning to hire workmen to work in his vineyard for the day. He made a deal with the men – the pay for working that day would be one silver coin called a denarius. Later that day, around nine in the morning, he noticed some men standing idle in the market place. He said to them, 'Go and work in my vineyard. I will pay you a fair wage.' The men agreed.

At twelve o'clock and again at three o'clock he did the same thing.

At nearly five o'clock he saw men loitering in the market place. 'Why are you wasting your time? Why are you not working?' he asked. 'Nobody hired us,' they replied. 'Well, go and work in my vineyard,' he told them.

At six o'clock, as darkness fell, work stopped for the day.

'Call the workers together and pay them their wages,' the owner ordered the foreman.

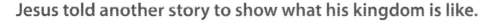

49

'Start with those who were hired last.' The men who started work at five o'clock and worked for one hour were paid one silver denarius.

The men who were hired first thought to themselves, 'We will get much more than them. We have worked for longer.'

When their turn came, they too were given one silver denarius. They took the money with bad feeling and immediately complained. 'We have worked far longer than these other fellows who only started at five o'clock. We have had to put up with all the heat of the day. Why did we not get paid more?' they muttered.

'I have not cheated you,' the owner replied. 'You happily agreed to do the day's work for one denarius. I have the right to do with my own money, whatever I wish. You are jealous of my generosity to the others.'

Heaven is the reward that Jesus prepares for for his people. If we turn from our sin and trust the Lord Jesus we will be in heaven at last with him. Heaven is a place of perfect happiness – for those who live a long life as Christians and for those who have only become Christians shortly before their death. The reward is the same. Yet we should not be tempted to put off this important matter until we are old.

Nobody can be sure of the future.
Now is the time to trust the Lord Jesus.

The Good Samaritan

Luke 10:25-37

One day a smart lawyer asked Jesus a difficult question.

'Teacher, what should I do to inherit eternal life?'

Jesus responded by asking two more questions:

'What is written in the Law? How do you read it?'

The lawyer thought he knew the right answer. 'You shall love the Lord your God with all your heart and with all your soul, and with all your strength and with all your mind, and your neighbour as yourself,' he replied.

'You have answered correctly,' Jesus said. 'Do this and you will live.'

However, the lawyer had another question. 'Who is my neighbour?'

Jesus answered him with a story.

A man was travelling from Jerusalem to Jericho. This was a dangerous and lonely route. He was attacked by a band of robbers, who stripped him of his possessions and beat him up. He was left at the roadside half dead.

First on the scene was a priest – a religious man who worked in the temple. Surely, he would help. No, he didn't. He hurried on by on the other side of the road. Next to come along was another temple worker – a Levite. He looked at the injured man, but also hurried away.

Then a Samaritan arrived. Now Samaritans usually had nothing to do with Jewish people. They had fights and quarrels stretching back for generations.

However, when the Samaritan saw the poor man lying there, he had pity on him. He bandaged up his wounds and even put the man on his donkey and brought him to an inn where he cared for him overnight. The next morning he gave the innkeeper a generous sum of money. 'Take care of this man,' he said. 'If you spend any more, I will repay you when I pass this way again.'

Jesus asked the lawyer another question. 'Which of these three (the priest, the Levite or the Samaritan) do you think was a neighbour to the man who was attacked?'

'The one who showed him mercy,' the lawyer replied.'

'You go and do the same,' Jesus told the lawyer.

Showing kindness to others will not earn us salvation, but it will show if we have love for the Lord Jesus.

The Lord Jesus, the Son of God, came to this world to live a perfect life and die on the cross, bearing the punishment for the sins of all those who have faith in him.

We can show love to those we meet, our neighbours, because Jesus himself has placed that love in our hearts.

Let's Pray!

Ask God to show you how to glorify him with your life.

Ask him to help you obey his Word so the world will see you belong to him.

Thank God that he is in control of everything – now and in the future. Trust in him.

The Unforgiving Servant

Matthew 18:21-35

One day Peter asked Jesus a question.

'If somebody keeps on sinning against me, how many times do I have to forgive him? As many as seven times?'

'No, not seven times,' Jesus answered, 'but seventy times seven.'

We always have to be ready to forgive others. Jesus told a story to explain.

Once there was a king who decided to settle his accounts with his servants. Was there any money owed to him? One servant was brought to him who owed him a huge sum of money. The man did not have the money to pay his debt so the king ordered, 'Sell him as a slave with his wife and children. Sell all that he has.'

The man was extremely distressed. He fell on his knees and begged the king, 'Please be patient with me. I will pay you everything.'

The king felt sorry for him, so he forgave the debt and let him go.

When the man went out, he met one of his friends who owed him a small amount of money. He grabbed him by the neck and started choking him. 'Pay me back the money you owe,' he yelled.

His friend fell on his knees and begged him, 'Please be patient with me; I will pay you everything.' (These were the same words that he had used to the king not long before.)

However, the servant was not so kind and forgiving as the king. He had his friend thrown into jail.

When the king heard of what had happened, he was angry. He called the servant back. 'You are a wicked man. I forgave you all you owed me. Shouldn't you have done the same?' The king was so angry that he threw the servant in jail too.

God forgives the members of his kingdom for every sin when they repent and trust in the Lord Jesus. If we have been forgiven so much, we should also forgive other people who do or say things against us.

A Persistent Widow

Luke 18:1-8

This parable of Jesus teaches us that we should never give up praying. We should never be discouraged.

There was a judge who only cared about himself. He did not bother about God or other people.

A poor widow had a legal problem and needed the judge's help. She came to him day after day asking him to do justice for her. For a long time he refused her requests. Eventually he decided to do something to help the woman.

'I do not care what happens to this woman, but she is becoming a nuisance. I had better do something before she wears me out completely.'

The unjust judge eventually listened to the persistent widow.

God will listen to those people coming to him in prayer, asking for his help. Jesus wants us never to give up praying.

A Loving Father

Luke 11:9-13

Jesus encouraged people to pray to God.

'Ask and it will be given to
you,' he said. 'Seek and you
will find; knock and the door will
be opened to you.'

He told a story about a father and his little boy.

'If a boy asks his father for a fish to eat, would the
father give him a snake instead?'

'If he asked for an egg, would he be given a poisonous scorpion by a loving father?'

Never.

'So,' said Jesus, 'if a sinful man wants to give good things to his child, how much more will God, the loving Father in heaven, give the Holy Spirit to those who ask him.'

The Holy Spirit will help us to understand the Bible and will show us how to serve Jesus and his kingdom.

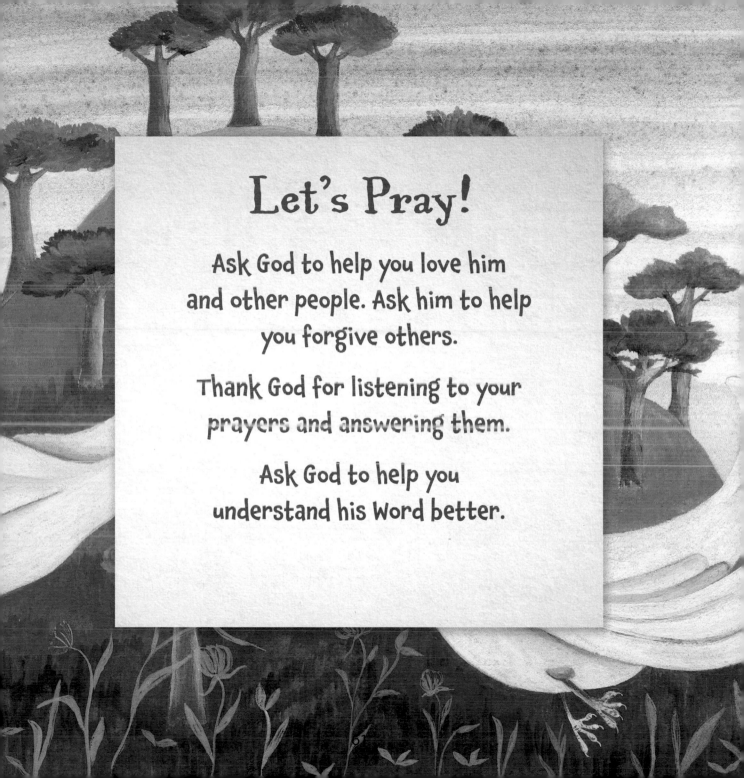

Let's Pray!

Ask God to help you love him and other people. Ask him to help you forgive others.

Thank God for listening to your prayers and answering them.

Ask God to help you understand his Word better.

Jesus and his Kingdom

Jesus told all these stories to teach his listeners about God, about the Bible and about how to live in obedience to God and his Word.

These stories teach us today too. They tell us about God and Jesus and his kingdom.

Many of the people who heard these stories first, turned their back on Jesus and did not believe him.

However, some did believe that Jesus was the Son of God, the great teacher who came to save his people from their sins.

It is the same today. Some people turn away from Jesus and reject his teaching, but God has worked in the hearts of many. They love God because he first loved them.

When we are drawn to Jesus by faith, he becomes our Saviour and the King of our lives.

Jesus' parables are all interesting stories, but each one teaches an important lesson.

Jesus wants us to know that God loves the world so much that he sent him, his Son, here to live the perfect sinless life for us and to die on the cross in our place.

Those who know and love Jesus as their Saviour, belong to his kingdom and want to obey him. We fall short and go astray many times, but the loving Father welcomes us back because of Jesus, our Lord and King.

Christian Focus Publications

Christian Focus Publications publishes books for adults and children under its four main imprints: Christian Focus, CF4K, Mentor and Christian Heritage. Our books reflect our conviction that God's Word is reliable and Jesus is the way to know him, and live for ever with him.

Our children's publication list covers pre-school to early teens. We also publish personal and family devotional titles, biographies and inspirational stories that children will love.

From pre-school board books to teenage apologetics, we have it covered!

Christian Focus Publications Ltd, Geanies House, Fearn, Ross-shire, IV20 1TW, Scotland, United Kingdom.

www.christianfocus.com

CHRISTIAN FOCUS PUBLICATIONS

Christian Focus   Christian Heritage   CF4K   Mentor

Endorsements

"No portion of Scripture captures the imagination and moves the heart like the parables told by Jesus. Simple enough for a child to understand, yet profound in what they teach, these accounts are earthly stories with a heavenly meaning. Carine MacKenzie has done every family a wonderful service in writing this children's book that I am sure will open the eyes of many to the glorious truths of the kingdom of God."

Anne Lawson, Wife of Dr Steven J. Lawson, (OnePassion Ministries, Trinity Bible Church of Dallas), mother of four, and grandmother to Charlotte

The parables told by the Lord Jesus Christ convey profound eternal realities in a direct everyday manner. This collection of Christ's parables is accompanied with simple prayers, helpful applications, and engaging illustrations. I trust it will be used to share the wonders of God's love and grace with many children.

Sharon James, The Christian Institute, UK.